AUG   2013

Fun with
FABRIC

Annalees Lim

WINDMILL
BOOKS
New York

Published in 2013 by Windmill Books, An Imprint of Rosen Publishing
29 East 21st Street, New York, NY 10010

Editor for Wayland: Victoria Brooker
US Editor: Sara Antill
Designer: Lisa Peacock
Photographer: Simon Pask
US Book Layout: Greg Tucker

Library of Congress Cataloging-in-Publication Data

Lim, Annalees.
 Fun with fabric / by Annalees Lim.
     p. cm. — (Clever crafts)
Includes index.
ISBN 978-1-4777-0180-5 (library binding) — ISBN 978-1-4777-0188-1 (pbk.) —
ISBN 978-1-4777-0189-8 (6-pack)
1. Soft toys—Juvenile literature. 2. Puppets—Juvenile literature. I. Title.
TT174.3.L56 2013
745.592'4—dc23
                              2012026230

Manufactured in the United States of America

CPSIA Compliance Information: Batch # BW13WM: For Further Information contact Windmill Books, New York, New York at 1-866-478-0556

Contents

Fun with Fabric

If you think having fun with fabric means sewing and stitching, think again! There is so much you can make with materials such as felt, buttons, and yarn without even threading a needle.

Small scraps of fabric, spare beads, and buttons can be easily found around your home. It is a good idea to keep them all together so when you are in the mood to make something, you can find them easily. Try storing them in an old shoebox and decorate it in a similar way to the books on page 14.

To keep your crafts nice and clean, always work in a clear area and put down a table covering first, especially if you are using glue. Material is a little harder to cut with scissors than paper so ask an adult for help.

In this book, you will need:

Felt
Lots of different colors.

Buttons
Extra buttons can usually be found on most clothes. Ask an adult to help you find them.

Fabric
Use old clothes instead of throwing them away.

Glue
We use fabric glue in most of these projects, because it is stronger for sticking materials together.

Scissors
Ask an adult to help with any tricky parts.

Finger Puppet Kingdom

Create a kingdom at your fingertips full of kings, queens, princes, and princesses, protected by brave knights.

You will need:
Scrap paper or cardboard
Pen
Different colored felt
Fabric glue
Scissors

1

Draw your finger puppet template onto a piece of scrap paper and cut it out.

2

Use the template to draw onto two pieces of felt. Cut out these shapes.

3

Glue the shapes together leaving the flat edge open so that your finger can be placed inside.

4

Cut out two circles for hands, two ear shapes, and two eyes.

Once you have made one finger puppet you can make any character you can think of. If you are stuck for inspiration, think of your favorite story or nursery rhyme.

5

Make a king by cutting out a crown, red robes, hair, and a mustache. You can cut out different shapes to make the rest of the puppets!

Fun Felt Veggie Patch

You will need:
Different colored felt
Scissors
Glue
Wooden stick
Plastic container
Googly eyes

You don't have to be an expert gardener to create your very own vegetable patch. These fun veggies are simple to make and even easier to keep!

1

To make peas in a pod, cut out a green ellipse shape and two thin curved shapes.

2

Glue a wooden stick into the middle of the green ellipse.

3

Cut out three light green peas and glue to cover the stick.

4

Glue the curved shapes onto the edge of the ellipse, covering the sides of the peas.

5

Glue the eyes onto the peas and leave to dry. Use the same technique to make more veggies. Roll some brown scrap felt into the container to stand your veggies in.

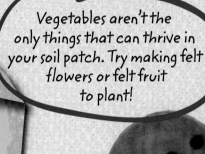

Vegetables aren't the only things that can thrive in your soil patch. Try making felt flowers or felt fruit to plant!

Braided Pals

You will need:
Fabric
Scissors
Yarn
Glue
Googly eyes

Create these funky fabric snail friends with just some scrap material, yarn, and a set of fun googly eyes.

Cut three pieces of fabric to the same width and length.

Tie the three pieces together with a knot.

Cut the short ends in two and wrap each section with yarn to make antennae.

4

Braid the long pieces together.

Try making a lovely, spotty ladybug or a creeping, crawling spider with this braided pals technique.

5

Roll the braided end up until it reaches the top and glue in place. Glue some googly eyes onto the knot to make your snail's face.

Woven Art

Have fun making this stunning woven art panel that looks great hung up on any wall.

You will need:

Piece of cardboard
Yarn
Scraps of material
Scissors
Black construction paper

1

Cut triangle grooves out of the short ends of the cardboard.

2

Wind the yarn around the cardboard using the grooves as a guide. When you have covered the cardboard tie both ends of the yarn together to secure it.

Weave scraps of fabric in and out of the yarn until the whole board is full.

You can make many of these small woven panels, carefully remove them from the cardboard loom, and sew them together to make a cool rug or blanket for your bed.

5

4

Trim any long ends to neaten the weaving.

Fold the black construction paper in half and cut a heart shape. Open the cut paper out and glue this on top of your weaving to frame your piece of art.

13

Felt Pattern Book Cover

You will need:
A book to decorate
Different colored felt
Scissors
Googly eyes
Fabric glue

Decorate your old notebooks or school books with these fancy felt figures.

Your felt friends can be stuck onto nearly any surface by using your fabric glue. Try sticking them to bags, keepsake boxes, or school folders.

1

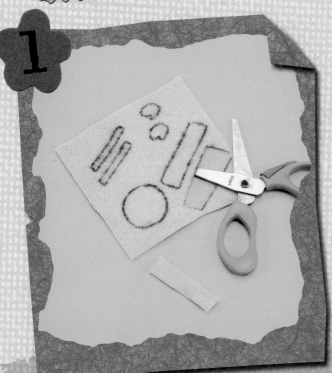

Cut a head, two arms, two legs, and two hands out of some felt.

2

Cut a T-shirt out of white felt and cut out red lines to make the pirate stripes and red shoes and a pirate hat.

3

Cut out some brown shorts, a black eye patch, and a silver sword.

4

Glue all the pieces onto the book using fabric glue and finish off the face with the black eye patch and a googly eye.

5

Surround your pirate with some yellow stars. You could create different felt characters for some other books.

Sock Monsters

You will need:
- Old socks
- Cushion stuffing
- Pipe cleaners
- Googly eyes
- Fabric glue

Shape and mold your very own mini monsters out of old socks and pipe cleaners!

1

Stuff your old, but clean, sock with the cushion stuffing until it is nearly full.

Mini monsters can be made from any items of clothing you are about to throw out. Cut off sleeves from an old sweater and sew up one end, or stuff an old wool glove.

2

Poke the open end inside your sock to keep the stuffing secure.

3

Tie a pipe cleaner around its middle to create a head. Glue two googly eyes of different size onto the head using some fabric glue.

4

Carefully cut two holes at the top of the head. Push a pipe cleaner through them to make antennae.

5

Cut small holes either side of the sock monster. Cut a pipe cleaner in half and push a half through each side to make some arms.

17

Button Buddies

You will need:
Elastic
Measuring tape
Scissors
Buttons

Don't let the spare buttons you have lying around and hidden in drawers go to waste! Build your very own button buddy that you can carry around with you or hang on your bag!

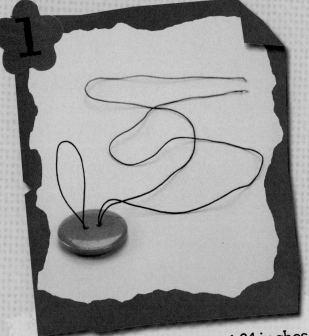

1

Cut a piece of elastic about 24 inches (60 cm) long and fold in half. Thread the folded end through the holes of a large button and tape in place.

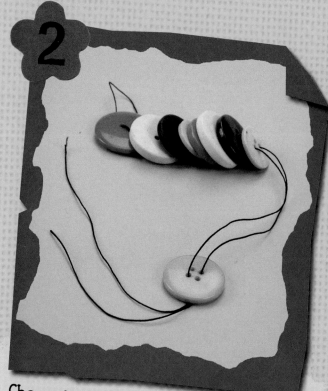

2

Choose ten buttons for the body and thread them on to the elastic.

3

Thread about 12 buttons onto each strand to make the legs. Tie a knot to secure in place.

Try making your buddies with different sizes and colors of buttons. You can take buttons from old clothes, but remember to ask an adult beforehand.

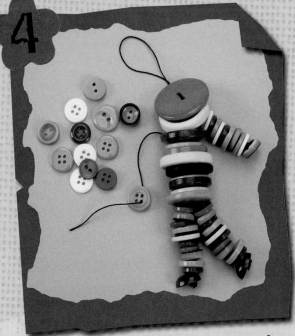

4

Cut a piece of elastic about 12 inches (30 cm) long. Thread about 20 buttons onto this. Tie at the ends and then tie it beneath the head to make the arms.

5

Glue some googly eyes onto the head to bring your button buddy to life!

Pom-Pom Pals

You will need:
Compass and pencil
Cardboard
Scissors
Yarn
Googly eyes
Felt
Fabric glue

Create cute pom-pom pals
for you and your friends
using scrap yarn and some felt.

1

Use your compass to draw two large
circles of the same size onto some
cardboard. Draw a smaller circle on
each and cut out.

2

Place these two rings together. Tie some
yarn onto the circle and loop the yarn
around it. Keep winding until you have
at least three layers.

Cut though the yarn in between the two rings. Slide some yarn between the cardboard and tie a knot. Remove the cardboard rings.

Glue googly eyes onto the pom-pom. Cut some feet and a nose out of some felt and glue these on.

Don't worry if you don't have a whole ball of yarn to use. Pom-pom pals can be made using scrap pieces of yarn to make a multicolored pom-pom pal!

Make some ears out of felt and stick them to the top of the pom-pom with fabric glue.

Pet Pouches

Keep your treasures safe with a pet pouch. Decorate these simple drawstring pouches with your favorite animal.

You will need:
A rectangle of fabric
Fabric glue
Scissors
Felt
Googly eyes
Ribbon

1

Make these pouches any size you like. Small pouches can be used to store jewelry or as party bags and bigger pouches can be used as a book bag.

With the fabric facing the right side toward you, put glue down one side and the bottom. Fold in half, press together and leave to dry.

2

Turn the material inside out so that the right side is on the outside. Fold down 1 inch (2.5 cm) of material from the top. Cut 2 triangles 1 inch (2.5 cm) from the edge.

3

Cut some features out of felt to make your animal. For a rabbit, you will need two ears, cheeks, whiskers, nose, and teeth.

4

Glue the felt onto the pouch with fabric glue. Add some googly eyes.

5

Thread the ribbon in and out of the holes at the top of the pouch and pull together. Tie the ribbon in a bow to secure the pouch.

Glossary

ellipse (ih-LIPS) A shape that looks like a flattened circle.

inspiration (in-spuh-RAY-shun) An idea that encourages you to do or make something.

keepsake box (KEEP-sayk BOKS) A box where you can keep things that are special to you.

technique (tek-NEEK) The particular way of doing something.

template (TEM-plut) A pattern used as a guide for drawing or cutting.

weaving (WEE-ving) To make by passing fabric or threads over and under each other.

woven (WOH-ven) A piece of weaving.

Index

Websites

For web resources related to the subject of this book, go to:
www.windmillbooks.com/weblinks
and select this book's title.

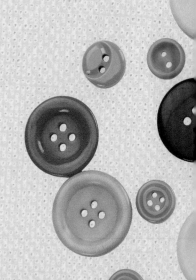